THE LAST DAYS OF HITLER

HUGH TREVOR-ROPER (Lord Dacre of Glanton) was born at Glanton, Northumberland, and was educated at Charterhouse and Christ Church, Oxford, where he read classics and modern history. From 1937 to 1939 he was a Research Fellow of Merton College, and subsequently a Student of Christ Church and University Lecturer in History. He was Regius Professor of Modern History, University of Oxford from 1957 to 1980, and Master of Peterhouse, Cambridge from 1980 to 1987. His books include *Archbishop Laud, Religion, the Reformation and Social Change, The Hermit of Peking, Renaissance Essays, Catholics, Anglicans and Puritans* and *From Counter-Reformation to Glorious Revolution.*